MERINDILOGUN FOLKTALES

MORALS OF YORUBA ODUS RELATING TODAY'S LIFESTYLES

VOLUME 2 SELECT ODUS

By Nia Jones-Morgan Oṣun Yami

Cover Design & Illustrations
By Luanne Ward
OnlyDefDesigns.com

ISBN: 9798672443881

Table Of Contents

This book is dedicated to my God daughters who afforded me the opportunity to live first hand through the Powers of the Three Great Goddesses.

Diane Smith-AdeLayo my Yemaya

Doreen Ward- OṣunTomi my Oṣun

Nyota Thacker- OyaKunile my Oya

Acknowledgements

From the bottom of my heart I salute all of my elders those whose shoulders I have leaned upon as well as all those whom I have not had the honor of meeting.

I salute my godchildren, those I have crowned and those who are walking on the road to oṣa, as this journey has been a reciprocal learning experience which I hope to carry on with them all for many more years.

I salute my children and all my other family members as you have all given me lots of love and let me know that this life is so very worthwhile.

I salute all of you who read these books as it allows me to know that I am helping to carry on this tradition in my small way. I would be remiss if I did not give thanks those who inspired me and kept me from wandering in doubt and fear when writing this book.

Thank you, thank you, thank you to the two ladies who from the very beginning of this journey graciously and lovingly gave me support, Yeye Luisah Teish and Iya Atilah Kadijah Wilson.

And of course to Baba John Mason who told me that my creativity is really what matters.

Iya Deborah Oguamah hunted me down to offer some very vital information.

I give thanks to my dear friend, Mr. Charles Short, my Task Master for teaching me about the need to purify my heart.

I must also give thanks to the two ladies, Jeanette Williams- Okan L'Onyin and Shereka Osario- OmiSaide whose eyes and ears helped to fine tune this project.

And last but not least, my heart goes out to that creative genius and editor, Luanne Ward who worked with me even in the wee hours of the night to make this a project of love.

Prologue

Yoruba? Isn't that the religion where they sacrifice chickens? You mean to tell me that you would write a book about it? Most definitely. It is long past the time that the world begins to understand and acknowledge the powerful contributions of the peoples of African descent. The principles and laws formed through the life and culture of the peoples of Africa has deeply and richly impacted the beauty and richness of our world today. It is the laws and principles of Ifa and Merindilogun that have served as shaping factors and have preserved the ancient teachings of our ancestors, egun and orișa. There are hundreds of thousands of practitioners of the African religion throughout the entire world. Somehow the truth has been withheld. This marks the era when Yoruba/ Orișa is set to step out and be seen in the world to assist with the transformation of mankind. It is now that the world will see how the ancient teachings have been interwoven into the life, culture and religions of peoples on every continent of this earth. Like all religions, Yoruba tenets have been passed down through what we call 'word of mouth'. It has only been in the last century that the stories and laws of the Yoruba peoples has appeared in written form. Today however, there are many books available relating to the history of this rich and colorful culture. So, let me ask you, don't you think it's time to shed light on the misconceptions that the so called 'powers that be' have erroneously perpetrated against the most profound belief system in the world?

As I reflect on the teachings that I have received over the past 27 years, this is my small contribution. Enjoy this project of mine. Have fun with it. Use it as you might find it to be a helpful tool towards your spiritual growth.

Moferefun Orişa
Nia Jones-Morgan Oşun Yami

Patakis of Selected Omo Odus

ÒWÁNÍ SÒBER÷ÒGÚNDÁ 11÷3 & ÒKÀNÀ÷ÈJÌÓKÓ 1÷2

The Odu **Owani Sober: Ogunda- 11:3**, talks about your clothes, or your appearance. But so does **Okana:Ejioko-1:2**. The underlying principle in both of these odus is TRANSFORMATION. One saves you from death and the other causes your death. Let's first take a look at the one that causes your death.

Okana: Ejioko- 1:2
The pataki referred to here is where two brothers were always embroiled in arguments. They constantly argued about which one was smarter, better looking, or better dressed. The first one always wore black clothes and the second one always wore white clothes. The first one said to his brother, "No one can kill you as long as your Orişa doesn't permit it." The second brother responded by saying, "Obatala is the one who rules my head and protects me. And he reigns over all other orişa and no matter what I wear, Obatala will always protect me." As usual, his brother disagreed. One day they both went to Obatala's house to try and settle their argument to ensure that Obatala reigns over all others. The second brother, who disagreed with what his brother stated in the beginning, told Obatala what the first one said to him. Obatala wanted to prove him wrong so he told him to invite his brother to go to the mountain in 3 days. Obatala decided to talk to Ososi about this matter. Obatala went to Oşosi's domain in the Upper Heavens and told him to go to the mountain and when the

brothers arrive, kill the one dressed in black. The second brother felt uncomfortable about his arrangement and decided to go to Orunmila for ebo before going to the mountain. Orunmila advised him to find a way to convince his brother to change clothes with him.

The day came when they were to go to the mountain. But even then, as usual, on their way they could not stop arguing with each other. Just before reaching the mountain, the second brother on a dare tricked him and was able to convince his brother to exchange clothes with him. Oṣosi saw the brothers approaching and as he was told by Obatala, he took his bow and arrow and killed the one dressed in black. The second brother went back to Obatala and told him his brother was killed. Obatala was stunned. His planned back fired. He thought about what the second brother had told him earlier and agreed, "No one can kill you as long as your Oriṣa doesn't permit it with ebo."

Here, two brothers argue about who is better. Not only who is better, but who is better protected. In this odu, Elegba is the reigning oriṣa. You are faced with family setting you up then selling you out for their own gain. 'Tattle Tailing' can be dangerous. Here you are gullible and not paying attention to what is being said and done. You are accepting advice that makes you change your mind, your way of doing things, your signature or even, your head. So much so, that you swallow the osogbo of your family member. Leti obitele, listen, listen and pay attention.

The argument was settled at the expense of the demise of one brother. Obatala warned them to go to the mountain. This is the place where you go to meditate to gain an understanding of what is transpiring in this situation. Unfortunately, by not thinking, you were knocked out of your center and bamboozled to transform and change your basic way of functioning and were sold out.

Owani: Ogunda- 11:3

When I picked up my notes, I found that the **Odu Owani: Ogunda-11:3** had an interesting message about appearances as well. It talks about how your style of clothes tends to represent your personal lifestyle, your personal brand, your personal signature. But it warns that in this instance, being easily identified is a disadvantage. Because in this odu, you want to be noticed and you want to function in an external environment but you may not have a strong enough inner support mechanism to protect you from the negative forces. You may be striving for heavenly things but in the interim, you will burn your wings. So in this odu, it's good to be conscientious but with modesty. At least until you develop the proper support. Until then, stick to tradition!!! Here, it shows that for one reason or another, you have enemies. There is a need for you to change your appearance, be unpredictable. Hide your intentions so that you don't become prey. ***As illustrated in this apataki, the Leopard whose spots were detectable from a mile away, dressed*** *in red making him even more unique in his appearance. He knew that it was the hunting season and that he, along with the other leopards were being hunted. He decided to go to Orunmila for ebo. Orunmila told him that he must change his clothes and camouflage himself. In so doing, his enemies would not recognize him and he would be saved. The next day he was about to leave the house and his wife called him back to remind him that he must take off his red cloth and change his clothes. He did and wore a cloth that concealed his spots. Now, the hunters couldn't identify him as a leopard and his life was no longer in jeopardy.*

In this case he wore clothing that was flamboyant for his social class or status. Years ago someone once told me that the sparrow can't hang out with the condor. It seems that he had high aspirations that he sought to set him apart from all the others. This odu warns you of being conspicuous. Don't tell your plans. Make unscheduled visits. Often change your route of travel. Ask Elegba for protection on your road.

ÒSÉ ÒDÍ
5 7

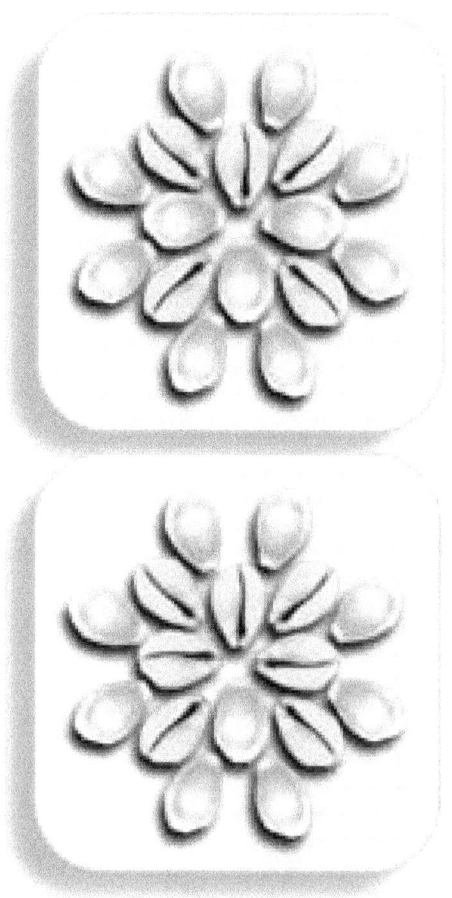

The Odu Ose: Odi-5:7 has been drifting in and out of my mind for the past 2 days. But there are 2 very important patakis associated with this odu that I feel need to be discussed. So I'm sitting here doing this 'eeny meeny miney mo' thing trying to decide whether to discuss the one about 1) 'paying what you owe' or 2) 'preparing for war'. Well, the 'war' won out.

In this odu, the land suffered from drought and very little crops were produced. As a result, the people were experiencing a period of famine. Orunmila constantly heard the cries of the young and old. Everyone prayed for rain. Orunmila divined and then called a meeting of the town folks and announced that the heavens are going to open up and rain cowries. Cowry shells were used as the currency so the entire town ran out into the streets with large baskets to catch the cowries. Orunmila did not go. Months went by and the town folks were enjoying their fortune. They were 'living high off the hog' so to speak. But then Orunmila divined again. This time he called a meeting and announced that the heavens ae going to open up and rain guns, axes and machetes. This time Orunmila was the only one to go out in the streets. The others were too busy living luxuriously and enjoying their fortune. So he collected all of the weapons. A neighboring village heard of the good fortune experienced by the town folks and wanted to control their riches so they declared war. The town folks were totally unprepared for war. They had no weapons of defense but they remembered that Orunmila had an arsenal. They all went to Orunmila for weapons.

Orunmila told them that they had to bring him all of the cowries as payment. Now Orunmila had both the weapons and the money.

Here it talks about a few issues that need exploring. Some books refer to this verse as, 'Prepare for War'. But it isn't simply preparing for war. It's about how you prepare for adversity. It's about assessing your resources and strategizing how to safeguard your valuables and your values. Why the suffering? Here there is a period of stagnation and debt but what are you doing? Getting out of debt takes more than wishful thinking. It's not going to fall from the sky into your lap. What about using your creativity? In this odu one has a great potential but no initiative to achieve. Ogun speaks in this odu. Don't rest on your laurels or take for granted the resources you already have. It's time to work hard for fulfillment. Orunmila is constantly engaged in this odu. In preparation, you must know the cycles of life. Know that whenever the elements are up, there has to come a time when they must go down, so prepare. Here, even when warned, you are impressionable but have a contracted sphere of awareness. There are no laws of time to help regulate your life. In times of war or when adversity is upon you, WILL victory. Understand that Oṣun appears in this odu bringing riches and resources. Present her with gifts. The objective is to win but it's the journey and how you function on its path that colors your personality. My Godfather of Warriors, John Mason said, "Victory is not an act of Completion but one of Becoming". The lesson is in preparing and creating the means by which you reach that end. It's about defining the YOU element through your experiences whether they are richer or poorer.

ÈJÍLÁ SÒBER ƆÒSÁ
12:9

Ejila Sober: Osa- 12:9- is an odu where because of the feeling of ENTITLEMENT, Oya finds it necessary to blow her powers through a situation to initiate a revolution that ultimately becomes an evolution. So of course Ogun and Ṣango step in here because those feelings and beliefs of entitlement result in wrong patterns of thinking about life in general and must be changed. Let me illustrate this concept through this apataki.

Orunmila overheard his neighbors talking about how the land of ekute (rats) was being overrun with robbing, looting and all types of degradation. Given the fact that they were in such close proximity to that town, he decided to make a visit. When he arrived, he saw that what he had heard was true. Much to his dismay, it wasn't the eku (street mice and rats) that were out of control. It happened to be the ekute (house mice and rats) that were at fault. These were the ones that at one time lived high off the hog. So he questioned himself how and why could this happen? What caused this unfortunate change of status? After doing a little investigating, he came to the conclusion that this was due simply to laziness and a lack of initiative. They felt entitled to be House rats not Field rats. Orunmila called them all together and gave them an ebo that would change their sedentary habits. But at that meeting, they explained that they didn't need his advice and that they were fine living exactly as they were. They then told Orunmila to leave them alone and he did.

But when he left, he went straight to the land of the ologbo (cats). This is the town where they were constantly working hard to provide for their families. They always adhered to tradition and held their family values high. Orunmila told them that if they were to do an ebo of meat to Ogun, they would never have to suffer the hardship and toil again. They complied and Orunmila took them all to the land of ekute. Needless to say, that from that time on, they were now declared as the natural predators of ekute, you know the outcome.

So in this odu, you are warned that you may be displaced or replaced from your home, job, etc. Your creativity is missing. You are taking things for granted and need to make quick changes or there will be an upset in status quo. You need to bring a little of Şango's energy into the matter to get things going. It also tells the diviner that the client may not follow their advice. If so, leave them alone and they will learn through the school of hard knocks. In this case however, the total blame may not lie on the shoulders of the town folk (ekute). Perhaps they were not taught the skill or importance of how to succeed. They may not have had the proper skills or have been given the right approach to learn and utilize their resources. Nevertheless, an immediate and probably a forceful change is about to happen. Be careful.

MÀRÙNLÁ:ÈJÍÒGBÈ/ÈJÍÙNLÈ
15:8

Marunla: Ejiogbe/ Ejiunle- 15:8-is another Odu where Ṣango is needed to make a curtain call. But this time it's in support of one of Olokun's counterparts Olokun Sonde.

In this pataki, Olodumare only sent down a select few of the 401 oriṣas from the Upper Heavens to inhabit the earth. The chosen ones arrived and took their places. The others were comfortable knowing that when it was necessary, they would be called upon to instill their powers where and when they were needed. Olokun Sonde was one of the oriṣa that remained in the Upper Heavens but she had a deep, burning desire to go to earth and live in the seas by the side of Olokun. She was very unhappy and every day she cried, prayed, begged and pleaded to inhabit the seas but she was never given that permission.

Ṣango's emotional upliftment and courage is needed here.

As time went on, Olokun Sonde lost her initiative. Her heart was unstable and it hurt. She was consumed with sorrow and a longing desire to be in the sea. She believed that life was passing her by. She felt trapped and began to lose self-confidence because her reasoning was clouded by her emotions. In her dismay, she did not know what to do. As a last resort, she went to Orunmila for advice. He told her that no matter what, she will never obtain what her heart desired. She must learn to accept the station ordained for her. But she did not want to believe what Orunmila declared. She cried and begged him for an ebo.

Orunmila told her that she must gain control over her emotions and accept her station as it has always been a protective faculty over her existence. The sea is not her place no matter how much she desired to be there. However, he conceded after discussing her plight with the Orişa of the Upper Heavens and it was decided that since she had learned to withstand the attribute of patience, she would go down to earth but she would reign as the Queen of All Running Streams as it was deemed that she mastered the art of 'emotional endurance' and the use of the 'lines of least resistance'.

In this odu, you have defeated expectations however, your long awaited change will finally come to you but not violently as in the previous odu, **Ejila Sober: Osa-12:9**. In this odu your situation will change slowly like the running steam, so accept it. It may not be exactly what you intended, yet concessions have been made and 'It Is What It Is'. Keep in mind that it is not stagnant. Progress has been made. Also know that lessons of perseverance in the long run will bring you an honor of status.

ÈJÌÒKÒ:ÒGÚNDÁ

2:3

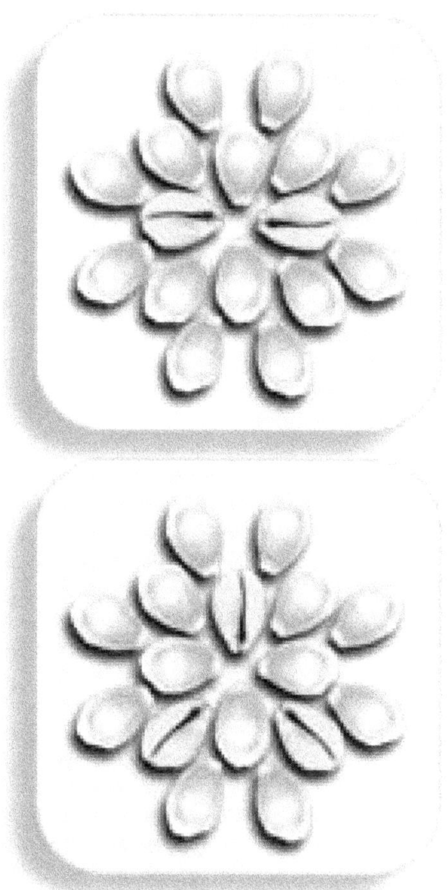

In the Odu **Ejioko: Ogunda-2:3**, there is a pataki that alludes to the egbe abiku. It talks about the sorrow that mothers endure as a result of improper care of twins. As such, the children, sometimes called the 'monkey children' would come to the earth plane then go then come and repeat the cycle. The orin, "obini mo ye edun, ibeji la omo odun" gives reference to this odu. **Ejioko:Ogunda-2:3**, is a deep odu. Some of the apatakis here portray stories that take place in the Upper Echelons of the heavens or within the portals of their depths. Their domain is where in some systems, is called in the Supernal Triad. This is the space where the griots consider the dwelling place of the omnipresent, omniscient and the omnipotent or the dwelling place of Olodumare, Odudua and Olorun. This apataki is filled with phenomenal secrets, but I've decided to discuss it in a later volume.

But, there is another apataki that I found to be interesting. It talks about the sorrow that the orişa Erinle endured. Erinle is sometimes called the 'Elephant of the Earth'. In fact, erin is the Yoruba word for elephant and according to people of Yoruba and Benin, the elephant is of Royal status.

In this apataki, Osoosi was a great elephant bounty hunter who acquired his fame because he proved to be the only marksman abled to capture the tusks of the elephants and present them to Odudua. Now it must be understood that Obatala, Olokun, Olofi nor any of the other orişa could accept ivory. Ivory is sacred and only

Odudua (the male aspect), Odua (the female aspect) and Olorun who dwelled in the Royal Heavens and were able to accept ivory.

Now, for some time, Osoosi would go out to hunt the elephant and unfortunately, he would wound them but the elephants would be able to escape and run to the other side of the river and hide in the high brush and reeds. No matter how much he tried to strategize and improve his acuity, the trajectory of his spears always missed the mark. He became distraught and decided to go to Orunmila for help. He was directed to make ebo and go to the far side of the river. Once there, he would be able to secure the riches and take them to the Royal Heavens. However, when he got to the edge of the river, he was bewildered because he had no way of getting to the other side. He was distraught because he tried and tried to regain his skill but to no avail. He became depressed, fell asleep and dreamed that his spears had turned to gold and were traveling through the air with the speed of light. When he woke up, he realized that it was just a dream. But he then gazed further down the river bank, and saw a man sleeping in a boat. He approached him and explained his dilemma. The man in the boat explained that he has not had any passengers for many days and he is grateful for the task. He carried Osoosi across the river and Osoosi was able to prove himself an excellent marksman and to recover his losses and take them to the Royal Heavens and finally present them to Odudua.

This odu asks, "How do you overcome anxiety and depression in order to pursue what you want when it is out of your reach?" Here, you must form alliances and associates to assist you in achieving your goals, but not just anyone. You must choose a skilled complement with whom to partner. You must ask, "How do I bridge the gap?" In this case, it was Aganju the Ferryman whose function is to teach you how to navigate through your emotions along your path from where you are to your destination. But before reaching that point, your anxiety or fears must be calmed in order to allow Divinity to show you the way. Falling asleep was tapping into the subconscious. Looking deeper into the symbolic representations within this odu we find Oṣun who served as a protective mechanism for the royal elephants of prey. It is the river with her many changes in the flow of emotions that must be overcome here. Coupled with the aid of Aganju, the Ferryman in his role of navigator through the channels, calmness and clarity of perception is found. This channel is the river of fear not the channel of anger as in his role of the volcano. There is also depicted the fundamental marriage between Aganju and Oṣun. And of course we have the boat which is Yemaya's sacred vehicle of water navigation.

MÈTÀNLÁ/ÌKÁ:ÈJÌOGBÈ/ÈJÌÚNLÈ

13:8

Metanla/Ika: Ejiogbe/Ejiunle-13:8

Being a daughter of Oṣun, I was always fascinated with the stories about her relationships with men. It seemed like she's had an affair with every male oriṣa in the Yoruba pantheon. Let's see, there's Ṣango of course and Ogun, Elegba, Aganju, Oriṣa Oko, Babaluaiye, What? Babalu? So, being my nosey self, I started to investigate and ran into the odu Metanla:Ogbe-13:8.

This is the Road of Oluo Popo. In this odu, Babaluaiye is dressed in sack cloth and wanders around carrying a wooden conical bell. He is destitute. Dirty, hungry and sick, he is looking for food and shelter when he comes upon the home of Ṣango's Oluwo. Everyone knows that Oluwos are rich and bountiful so Babaluaiye was relieved and full of hope that he could finally clean up, eat and rest. Upon reaching the door, he rang his wooden conical bell. But when the Oluwo saw this dirty vagabond, he told him to get away from his door and get off of his property. Needless to say, Babaluaiye was shocked, embarrassed, disheartened and furious. In retaliation, he cursed the Oluwo and told him that from this day on, he will suffer. He will lose all of his bounty. Even his live stock will perish. Well, sure enough, within a few weeks, the Oluwo had lost practically all of his riches.

Angrily, Babaluaiye went to Orunmila to divine. He was directed to ebo Elegba and Oṣun which he did. When he went to Oṣun, she took him in, bathed him and being her

From my understanding, it is the Babalawos that carry the wooden conical emblem. Are they considered bells? Could Babalu's anger resulted because he felt that despite his defenseless outward appearance, his possession of the wooden conical bell would clearly indicate to the Oluwo that he at one time held a high position and there was a need to preserve his inner dignity? In this odu, Babaluaiye is a wanderer in a strange land searching for self and hoping for a rebirth, a resurrection but in return, received contempt and insulting treatment. His expectations were based on ego. At this point in the cycle, he had not yet exemplified his true capability. It was Oṣun that helped his transformation. When this odu falls on the mat, it warns of an impending change of residence, job or position but there is a need to broaden your perception because your thoughts are naive and narrow minded and your plans are unrealistic. What you think of yourself and your abilities are not what others see you as. It is time for a serious self-examination. How do you present yourself to the outside world? And the thing is, you have the innate ability to do it all. Before moving into the next venture of your life, check to ensure that your plans are founded. Babaluaiye had all of the knowledge and power he needed. He was able to heal the town with an amulet even though he cursed it earlier. This is definitely a matter of STATUS within changing cycles. Orunmila must mark the necessary ebo here. Seek counsel.

ÈJÌOGBÈ / ÈJÌÚNLÈ : ÈJÌÒKÒ

8 : 2

There's a pataki in the odu Ejiogbe/Ejiunle:Ejioko-8:2 that focuses on how the attitudes of our youth can bring about dire consequences. It might not even be the attitudes of youth. For that matter, it can be the attitudes of unevolved, immature adults. When Ejiogbe hits the mat, the overall premise is one of a promise of greatness at some point in your development. As my godfather of Warriors, John Mason said, "Ejiogbe marks one who is favored". But along with that, your values must get clear. If not, your ego will bring down all kinds of mischief affecting your emotional and spiritual growth. Now couple that with Ejioko which can often refer to police (aselu) intervention. The consequences as I said can be potentially harmful. Let me illustrate this in this apataki:

There was a young boy named Asberebere/Astute Power who was quite smart. He was well educated but also quite mischievous and foolish. As a child, his parents imposed no discipline on him and allowed him to do and act any way he wanted. However, his acts of folly often got him into trouble. It finally came to the point where he felt that he needed to make a change. He was tired of getting so entwined in trouble so he decided to go to Orunmila for an ebo. Orunmila marked an ebo to Elegba and he carried it out.

Three days later, he was walking down the country road and had the urge to move his bowels. He came upon a grove of kola trees. To make himself comfortable, he hung his jacket and bag on a limb of the tree. When he finished, he didn't realize that some of the kola nuts had fallen into his pockets. Nor did he realize that in that area, kola nuts were sacred and anyone caught stealing them would be arrested and sentenced to death. He barely walked a few yards when the police accosted him and he was arrested.

While in jail he prayed but could not understand why even after the ebo he did that he was to be executed. The day arrived that he was to be put to death. As he was led out by the guards, he began to sing and pray. Suddenly the sky turned dark and a loud clap of thunder and lightning filled the air almost striking the guards. They were so frightened that they panicked and momentarily, loosened their hold on Asberebere. Once unshackled, he was able to escape.

What's interesting about this odu is that now there is an awakening or a period of self-awareness leading to an inevitable change in character. In the past, he didn't take life seriously. He was transforming as it was time to grow up. He was now ready to take on the burden of responsibility. In this apataki, he was vulnerable and left alone to walk through an unguarded territory. In addition, the process of transforming in this odu is symbolized by his defecation. He was getting rid of that which was no longer a part of him. It was a period of cleansing his toxic ways. It was about time for his spiritual growth and development. Elegba tested him.

The aselu came to impose discipline. Discipline is simply a system used to deter criminal or unacceptable behavior. Here, it's noted that if his parents imposed discipline on him as a child, he would then learn how to discipline himself. Therefore, at some point in life, discipline must be imposed. Unfortunately, it is often the police that carry it out. Godparents are chastised in this odu for not accompanying, teaching or protecting their Iyawos. There is a happy ending here. Ebo was done and Ṣango came in his defense because he was innocent. Another important issue in this odu is that Aseberbere was led on the path to find his destiny as a Babalawo. He was given the kola nuts as a sign of his impending Divinity.

ÈJÌOGBÈ/ÈJÌÚNLÈ:ÌROSÙN 8:4

Ejiogbe/Ejiunle: Irosun- 8:4- Whenever Ejiogbe falls on the mat it questions whether you know the value of your head. It states that with a kind heart, you have allowed yourself to be taken for granted and in some cases, taken advantage of. Follow your head before following your heart. But sell yourself. Learn how to use assertion instead of aggression in all of your undertakings. Then with balance you will not over step or under step your goals. Do not for one minute deny that awesome, wonderful, divine spirit within you regardless as to what others may say. The reason there may be struggle within relationships is because you don't sell yourself. You tend to be a very private person. There are layers of secrets with you. Therefore others make up stories of what they believe you are about. Most times, their stories have no credibility.

Now when Ejiogbe is coupled with Irosun, your perception is in question. Are you seeing clearly? Here there is a tendency to be mentally or emotionally paralyzed, spastic, frozen or disconnected. Actually, it can be termed procrastination. In this odu, you are supposed to step out and show the world who you are and what you are worth. You have a lot to offer. There's no need to fear. You are destined for greatness.

In relationships there may be a struggle between 2 high status heads vying for control. This is illustrated in the following pataki:

Orunmila and Olofi both lived in the Upper Heavens. Their domains were close to one another and they often talked about the deeds they performed for those that came for help. At times they would compare their deeds to see which one was more adept. But one day they got into a heated argument. Orunmila was bent on proving that he was smarter and more skillful than Olofi so he bet Olofi that he could grow toasted corn faster than Olofi could grow regular corn. Unknown to Olofi, Orunmila made a pact with Elegba to go into his fields at midnight of the New Moon cycle and replace ½ of his crops with toasted corn. He knew that at the New Moon, there is no light in the sky so Olofi would not be able to see (Irosun) what was happening in front of him. In addition, he went to Şango and asked his help by sending lightning flashes through the sky so that Elegba could see and carry out his part of the game. Once Elegba was able to scatter the toasted corn in the fields, Şango was then able to send rain to his crops. With the rain falling, by the 3rd day, shoots began to grow where the toasted corn was planted. Orunmila summoned Olofi for them to go out to investigate the progress of the crops. Due to the natural progression of growth, Olofin's crops did not begin to sprout. But when they went to Orunmila's crops, Olofi saw the toasted corn on the ground and had no choice but to submit to be defeated in their bet.

Orunmila used his head and won the bet. But it was through cunning. An issue that must not be overlooked is the fact that Olofi believed him. Here seeing is believing that events come about through truth even if it is a lie. Irosun says, even though you have the ability to see beyond sight, to intuit with clear perception what's on the spiritual plane, you fail to open your eyes and see what's really in front of you on the physical plane and not be bamboozled. Olofi opened himself to a competition but did not use his insight to sell himself. To develop his creative forces to make himself shine. Orunmila was shrewd and chose the New Moon because there would be limited ability to see clearly what was really going on. In this odu you are encouraged to FOCUS and then step out to manifest your greatness. No one else will do it for you!!!!!!

ÒBÀRÀ:ÒFÚN
6:10

Obara:Ofun-6:10. This odu speaks about status. It asks, how well do you administrate yourself? Are you sure that you are capable of maintaining a leadership position because here you are being held responsible for your reputation.

As illustrated in this apataki, Olofi's son was ill. At first he called all of the physicians in the town to treat his son. However, none of them were able to heal him. He failed to go to Orunmila for ebo. Instead, he called the Babalawo who lived at the edge of town to examine his son's condition. The Babalawo came with 2 assistants, Awo Osi and Awo Otun (his left and right hands). The Babalawo examined the boy then assured Olofi that his son would be cured. He was confident of his healing ability so he told his assistants to prepare the area for where the ritual would take place and call him when they were finished. His assistants were dedicated and wanted to make sure that everything was in perfect order for the Babalawo to begin. They took their time preparing making sure that everything was as it should be. When they finished, they notified the Babalawo that the space was ready. Ironically, when the Babalawo went to perform his healing ritual, it was too late as Olofi's son had died. Olofi was irate. He could not believe that his son was dead. He was so overwhelmed that he promised to punish the Babalawo. From that day on, that Babalawo could no longer practice healing. He could now only attend to the dead.

In this odu you may be good at planning, laying the foundation of power and mastery and even at initiating the tasks at hand. But overgeneralization coupled with overconfidence can cost you your job or your life. This issue points to the fact that you may have a responsibility which lies on your shoulders but instead of overseeing the project from the beginning to the end, you rely on others to assist you. Poor management due to overgeneralization is the problem. You may take into account that you assign your right hand man and your left hand man to help but you are needed to detail and ensure that balance is maintained throughout the entire situation. Based on this odu, inevitably, the responsibility lies on your shoulders. You can't blame your subordinates. Here you have a general understanding but you need details or disorder sets in. Your attention is relaxed. Exercise caution. First of all, inferior people must not be employed.

A lesson for diviners is, don't eat the osogbo of your clients or godchildren or Olofi will curse you. Know the implications of your act as you are complicit. Iku, Arun and Ofo speak here. It is suggested that you receive obe. Diabetes can affect the mind. Also be careful of high or low blood pressure. Get regular physical check-ups.

ÒGÚNDÁ:ÒSÉ

3:5

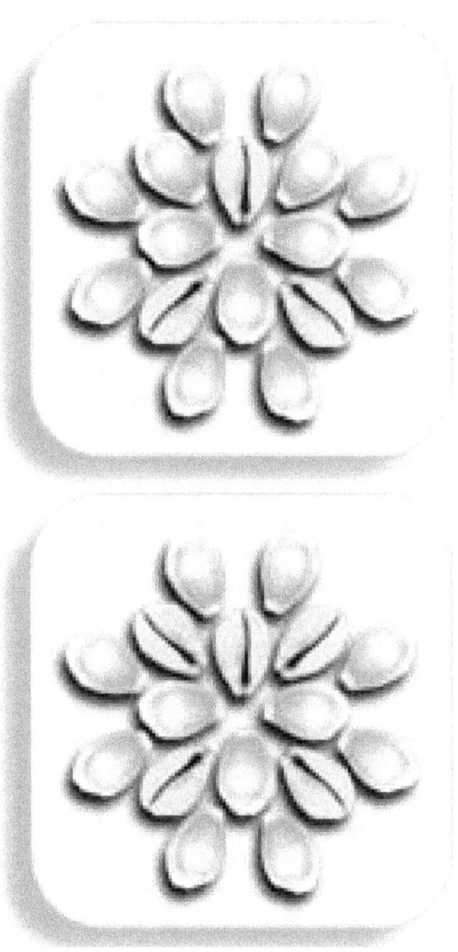

Here's another odu that I've been mulling over. It is **Ogunda:Ose-3:5**. There are many lessons to be learned from this odu but my favorite is the one where intrigue and distrust brings about a curse on women. Actually, that curse turns out to be a blessing for all mankind.

The apataki goes like this: There was an Awo who lived with his wife and he was a hunter. For weeks and weeks, he went out every day to capture game but failed. Both he and his wife wanted to know why food had become so scarce that he and his wife were starving. Finally, he decided to go to Orunmila for an ebo and was told to go to the Orisa of the Mountain, Obatala. On his way up the mountain he saw a peculiar Image among the trees. The Image summoned him over and told him a secret that must be kept. He said that from now on, as long as he kept the secret, he will find and capture his game. As the days went on, his wife was so surprised about this new turn of events. There were more animals captured than ever before. Food was in abundance. She was curious and asked her husband the Awo how did this come about? He would not disclose the secret.

She couldn't stand not knowing so one day, she put a hole in the bottom of his bag and filled the bottom with ashes. As planned the ashes fell out of his bag and she followed him. The Image saw her and became so angry that he called her to him and said, "since you are so curious to see the blood of the animals captured by your

husband, now you will be cursed and forced to see your own blood every month."

In this Odu, you are cursed for your curiosity and impetuousness. Reason being, you may be disappointed from unjustified expectations from a given situation. In relationships, men and women must work together like a pair of eyes. But here you feel lonely, unfulfilled and excluded. You begin to sneak around and become disloyal and untrustworthy. (It's like going through your mate's cell phone).

From a spiritual standpoint, her husband is an Awo which means secret. Secrets are private rites with penalties if dishonored. Don't go looking for what you're not entitled to see. Here, they are both seeking knowledge. Awo's objective is to open one's sphere of awareness. That is why Orunmila sent him to the mountain to seek counsel of the Orișa of Wisdom and metaphysical science. His wife was also seeking what he was seeking but instead was supposedly cursed. But here is born menstruation. With that came Fertility and the power to bear children and increase mankind on the earth plane. In this Odu, women are given human blood, THE PROFOUND POWER OF AȘE. That is the reason why so many women were burned at the stake and accused of being witches. Yes, as quiet as our secret is kept, we have THE ULTIMATE power of așe.

ÒDÍ ÒSÈ
7 5

Odi:Ose-7:5 is a very powerful odu as it marks the need to focus and adhere to that in which you are involved. In **Odi:Ose-7:5** folks have a tendency to allow curiosity to fuel temptation. Even though there is a lot of potential here, that curiosity is a complex emotional off shoot of wondering "What If?" But that "what if" tends to become a distraction which results in poor attention to the project at hand. So while you are wondering what's going on out there, you are not aware of the fact that you are in the process of being undermined by someone or something else. Things get waylaid. It may be due to impatience or possibly an attention deficit.

To illustrate this there is an apataki about the chicken who sits on her eggs and waits and waits and waits for them to hatch not concentrating on the process. Her mind is elsewhere. But much to her unknowing, there are parasites eating away at the eggs. After waiting so long, she tires and finally abandons her potential brood.

So…one must learn to pay attention to details. This odu lets you know that you are in a period of transition. This is the planning stage. Things are not organized or if they are, you have yet to experience the reality. There is still a need to gain a better perspective. You may start the work but can't finish. You may need help. But, check out your "friends". Be careful in order to avoid the infection of parasites (microscopic and macroscopic ones). There are those around you who drain your energy and are trying to usurp your power. Watch out for gossip.

When Odi appears in a reading with it comes the possibility that one may have stepped outside of what is considered 'traditionally acceptable' in some way. It may be something small or it can be considered a felony. Whatever the case, someone else knows about it and one can be 'busted'. The good thing about this is that no one 'saw' the offense. There is no 'proof'. Therefore, under this particular Odu one will be exonerated from the act. And again, this is about things that don't quite come to fruition. In this case, that's a good thing. But what about things that you seek to build and bring into fruition? What must be done?

Whichever it is, in this Odu, one must become mindful of the issue at hand or it will not blossom. Cultivate your endeavors. A very simple but beautiful Ebo given to me by my godfather of Warriors, John Mason, is to build a nest and in it, place all of your objectives. But meditate and pray on them while they develop.

ÒSÉ ÒFÚN
5:10

Ose:Ofun-5:10 is one of those Odus where no matter how you look at it, Iku (Death) or some aspect of it, is always the culprit behind the scenes. Here, one of the Owe Odus is called the Odu of Escape. But escaping what? Escaping Slavery and Death. Let me illustrate it in the following apataki:

Mama Pig and her children were housed in a pig sty along with many other pigs. She began to notice that every day the farmer would come and choose 2 young pigs to sell and slaughter. Fear for her children's lives took hold of her and she knew that she had to find a way to protect her young. She prayed and prayed until one day, Orunmila appeared to give her guidance. She explained her dilemma to him and he told her that he could not intercede with the farmer on her behalf as this was his livelihood and that because he did Ebo, he deserves what he receives from his business.

However, Orunmila decided to travel to Iku's domain and confront him. Iku was surprised to see that he had such an honored visitor and was quite curious as to the purpose of his visit. Iku and Orunmila had an in depth debate. Iku stated that he was simply the middle man who is being used in this business venture. He convinced Orunmila that his duty is an integral part of this business. Orunmila understood but explained that nevertheless, he is not to take Mama Pig or her children. Iku conceded but asked how would he know who they were? Orunmila said that they would be the ones wearing his Ide.

After putting the Ides on the family, Mama Pig gathered up her children and placed them in an area right next to the fence. She told them that under no uncertain circumstance are they to wander off or leave that area. She decided to inconspicuously and tirelessly dig a hole under the fence for her family to escape. She knew that the hole could not be so large that it could be spotted by the farmer or by her nosey, jealous neighbors. She also knew that her children were well fed and had become too fat to easily fit through the hole. What was she to do?

Every day when the farmer came to feed the animals, she would fast then ration the amount of food given to her children. Soon her children began to lose weight. Within a week, they were small enough to slip through the hole under the fence and escape from slaughter.

When **Ose:Ofun-5:10** falls on the mat it is important to know that Egun is warning that Iku is near. It is also important to acknowledge and elevate your ancestors as they are guiding and protecting you. Listen to them and if you are not able to hear them, you may need a spiritual Mass. In this Odu you are a creative challenger of authority. Authority in this case may be working against you with an intentional transgression. But it may not be with malice. You must be able to put yourself in their shoes, understand that it is not personal so forgive. But above all, take care of you and yours. Those working under you must learn to obey.

You are keen and willing to work diligently to accomplish your objectives. But even though you may have a clear mind, you must also have a clean, clear body. Know that in this Odu, your diet is very important. There may be a need to get rid of excess baggage. Sickness may be hiding within. So begin a cleansing diet as Babaluaiye speaks in this Odu. It is evident that not only are your ancestors protecting you but Orunmila protects you with his talisman. You must wear his Ide and perhaps receive Kofa. It was stated earlier that jealousy is surrounding you. As you move on and away implore your ancestors to keep you protected from harm in any form.

ÒGÚNDÁ꞉ÈJÌOGBÉ/ÈJÌÚNLÉ
3꞉8

Ogunda:Ejiogbe/Ejiunle-3:8. There are 2 odus I came across that describe how effective means of negotiation on the road is used to acquire what you need.
Ogunda:Ejiogbe/Ejiunle-3:8 and **Owani:Ejila-11:12.** The first odu has a pataki of which most folks in our religion are familiar.

Ogun had been working on a project for 3 days with little rest in between when he realized that he had not taken time out to eat. He set out on the road to find food when he saw man in the distance, sitting on the banks of the lagoon fishing. He decided to catch some fish for his meal. It wasn't long before he caught a huge fish. He was happy and grateful.

However, the man who had been sitting on the edge of the lagoon told him that he deserved the fish because he's been there for hours and believed it was unfair that a Johnny Come Lately could come by and take the fish he's been waiting for all day. They began to argue. The argument was getting out of hand. They were loud and it caught the attention of the owner of the lagoon. The owner told them both that given the fact that he is the owner, the fish should belong to him.
The 3 men argued long and hard until Elegba overheard them and went to Olofi so that he could intervene. Olofi came and listened to each one's point of view when finally he asked for the fish, took out Knife and cut the fish into 3 equal parts. Immediately the argument was squashed.

So in this case, it's not simply a matter of who is entitled to the bounty. Nor is it a matter of how the best opponent uses their wit to undermine the other's perceived rights. It is evident that there was improper assessment from the beginning. All three opponents have legitimate grounds (so they each think) for winning their case.

Unfortunately, even though they are sincere in their positions, it is their thoughts that are the problem. What is important is the fact that friendship and equal justice is more important than being right. Therefore, compromise is a must as they definitely lacked unity. But now even more than that, the most prevalent lesson in this odu was the fact that Olofi, the mediator, the unbiased one, introduced wisdom into the situation in order to bring about balance to conflict. For this odu, the ebo may be three smoked fish and 3 packets of aṣe to the river, lake or lagoon. Also, Obe may be needed.

ÒDÍ ÒBÀRÀ

7 6

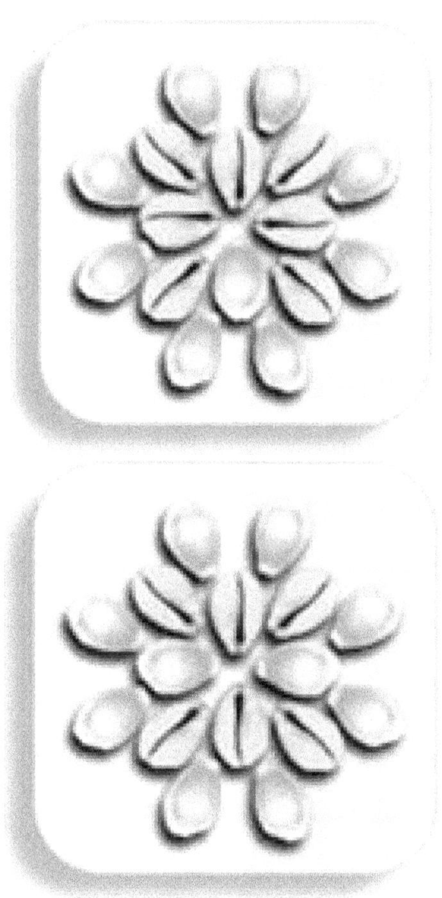

My godfather, Alfred Davis- Omi Toki -ibae tonu (whom I miss so very, very much) was a social worker and in some instances, knowing my background, in the private Merindilogun classes taught me from a clinical social work standpoint. For instance, he said when looking into the Odu Ose, the basic principle is emotional compensation. But looking into the Odu Odi, it is emotional complexes. So of course that spiked my curiosity. According to the American Heritage Dictionary of the English Language, 5th edition, complex emotions are thought forms that can be complicated, intricate, involved, interconnected, entwined and/ or interwoven. So now my question was, how does that play out in each Odi Odus? I found that with many of the readings I give to my clients, **Odi: Obara- 7:6** is an odu that tends to come up most often.

Odi: Obara- 7:6 talks about Indecision. Here you are presented with a myriad of possibilities yet the inability to discern which is most beneficial. You are faced with the question of which road to take? You are standing at the Fork in the Road and wondering do you go East, West, North, South, Northeast, Southeast, Northwest or Southwest? Where to venture next? This is truly an Elegba issue.

It is often said that Odi harbors issues of passion, adultery, sex abuse and lust. Fickle characteristics are found here. In **Odi:Obara- 7:6**, if it looks good, feels good, tastes good, you're down. This is where it becomes a complex issue because your reason is clouded by your emotionalism. You tend to OVER ASSESS. You go from one thing or person, to another then another. Everything or everyone looks good. Passion is up and you want it or them but which one?

There is an apataki that illustrates how at one time, women worked hard and lived in a town that was financially stable. They owned the marketplace and were the rulers of industry. They were self- sufficient. Now on the outskirts of town there was a camp of men marauders who would go out to war in neighboring towns. They raped, killed, stole and conquered but had no secure environment to house their bounty. In fact, they would encamp down by the river. However, one day the river overflowed and destroyed their goods so they were forced to relocate. They knew that there was a town where only women lived and believed that they could easily rape and over power them. Little did they know that the women trained themselves to be expert markspersons and were able to protect their environment. So when the marauders came upon them, they tried to convince the women to submit but to their surprise were met with a great protective force.

So, what next? The women had been without men for a long time and passion had built up. The men by their nature also had passion. But it wasn't even passion it had become lust that needed to be restrained. Both camps wanted the same thing, a sense of security within a protected environment and a need to work together to achieve that end, but should they and if so, how? Each group had to calmly weigh the conditions then prioritize their needs. Here meditation is the key. You must go to the center of your being to find the line of least resistance. Focus on your objective. Exactly what do you want and what are you willing to sacrifice? Use the peony eleke and a white candle to pray with. Draw up a petition or contract for yourself and/or others. No indecision, ambiguity or perplexity allowed at this point. In fact, this is the Odu of the Birth of Marriage. Laws of relationships are formed. As The Rock says, "Know your role!" and work within those boundaries.

ÒSÀ:ÒFÙN
9:10

Osa:Ofun-9:10. In almost all of these odus, I select one apataki to discuss. But here I am making an exception because there are 3 patakis in **Osa:Ofun-9:10** that are so significant that I feel a need to briefly mention all of them as an illustration of situations of betrayal.

The first apataki is known as the Odu of the Butterfly. So when I came upon this odu I immediately visualized its movements in order to feel its essence. What I felt was the beauty of its wings, the lightness of its spirit, the fragility of its body and the shortness of its lifespan. I pictured the transformation of its character being explicit in its total and complete metamorphosis. Its entire life is delicate yet easily taken advantage of by elements in the environment which in this odu, tend to be malevolent forces. *Butterfly thought to herself how difficult it had been for her to fight through the issues she encountered during her period of total transformation. It was the hardest ordeal that she would ever have to experience in her life. So she thought. For now, she felt light, beautiful and free in comparison to the old. She was at peace and felt joy with the fact that she could fly from the top of the trees to the bottom of the bushes. She could not believe how far she was able to fly. One day while in flight, she noticed in the distance that there was a city with tall buildings and lots of people. She challenged herself to go to see how people lived in the city. As soon as she arrived, she felt the smog and heaviness of the air. It was not light and sweet like it was when she was in the country. Suddenly, she felt a strong whirl wind approaching. She tried to fly as fast as she could to find shelter. She was able to hide under the ledge of a building. While there, she remembered how safe and secure she felt when she was wrapped in her cocoon. She prayed to Olofi that she would be protected from Oya's storm. She was afraid and vowed to return to the peacefulness of the country as soon as the storm subsided. When it was over, she began her trek back to the country. But on the way, the winds became strong and forced her to glide towards a park where children were playing. When they saw her, they ran after her and captured her. They did not handle her with care. She lost her delicate wings and soon perished.*

This pataki talks about how in its innocence, the butterfly thrives in the country but becomes bombarded by the heaviness of the city and the wickedness of the people. Because in **Osa:Ofun-9:10,** the butterfly goes to the city and is killed by the uncultured, undisciplined, ignorant children. A butterfly can't survive in Osa for long because as it hangs out in Yansa's domain, Yansa may act as the gentle wind for a while but at any moment, she can turn and wind those delicate wings to a pulp as in the orin (pa won, pa won, pa won oriṣa). Therefore, in this odu, dangerous elements may be sent to you. And like the wind, those forces may not be seen, only felt and in time, your ideas, dreams, objectives, plans and even your life can get caught up in the tornado and turn topsy-turvy and no good may come of it. Olofi is needed to ward off possible disintegrating forces.

There is another apataki where Obatala is betrayed by his close friend monkey. *Monkey and Obatala were good friends. Monkey was always on the move. He was a social being who would always come back and share his experiences with his friend Obatala. Obatala, on the other hand, was a peaceful, sedentary being. He was a thinker and enjoyed his life from encounters with the orisa. He enjoyed sharing stories about his experiences with Monkey and vice versa. One day, monkey was among his friends and found himself bragging about how he was entitled to know the secrets of what the orisa disclosed to Obatala. When asked about them, Monkey made up a story and said that Obatala disclosed it to him. His friends did not believe his story but in order to save face, he lied and casted a dark mark on his trusted friend Obatala.*

Monkey chatters and talks too much to others about Obatala. Inevitably, his stories misrepresent Obatala's character and in this odu, he lied and betrayed him. In this Odu, **Osa:Ofun-9:10**, you are warned about a friend that gossips and fabricates stories about you. Discretion is needed when it comes to trusting a friend.

Now, the third apataki is about competition and how people use their creativity and by any means necessary, cheat in order to get ahead especially when the odds are against them. For instance, *Dog and Turtle had been friends for many years. They often enjoyed their conversations together. They were familiar with one another's family and even on occasion planned outings together. However on this day, while they were having a discussion, Dog challenged Turtle to a race. Turtle thought it was all in fun and took him up on the bet. But Turtle knew that he could not possibly beat Dog in a race. So he went to Orunmila for an ebo. Orunmila instructed Turtle to get a bone and wrap silk thread around it then leave it in the middle of the road. Turtle obeyed. The race started but true to the character of a dog, when Dog came upon the bone, he couldn't resist eating it and playing with the thread. As a result, Dog became entangled in the thread and could not move. Needless to say, Turtle kept to his slow, steady pace and won the race.*

In this odu, you may find yourself in a situation that seems impossible to achieve. The physical, emotional, mental and financial odds are against you. But with perseverance and ebo, orişa and your spirit will create a way. There is a warning to be careful of defeated expectations.

Glossary

Abiku- A child who have been born to their mother and yet, lived for a short time, either as a child or a fetus. That child is then reborn to the same mother again. This can be a repeated phenomena many times.

Aboriṣa- One who has committed to the beliefs of oriṣa practice.

 Ade- One who wears a crown.

Adimu- An offering given to the oriṣa.

Agemo- An oriṣa who appears in the form of a chameleon.

Akuko- A male chicken.

Akara- A patty made from fried black eyed peas.

Aleyo- A non- initiated seeker of the Yoruba religion.

Amala- Porrige made from corn meal and okra.

Arara- Dahomey Africa land of Benin.

Aṣe- Universal Power.

Aṣo- Cloth.

Ayan- The sacred drums. AS Baba John Mason describes, tthey represent the Ultimate Expression of God as Sound, the Repository of Divine Power and the Vehicle to give it Voice. It is also made from the African Silk Tree.

Baba- Father.

Babalawo- The authority bestowed upon learned priests of Ifa upon initiation to the oriṣa Orunmila.

Babaloṣa- A male priest.

Calabash- Gourd, pumpkin.

Cowrie- Shells were used as money at one time. It is also used when casting for the Merindilogun.

Divination- A classification system that contacts entities of Orun, the Heavens to foretell information stored in Destiny.

Ebo- Sacrifice.

Efun- Chalk substance made from egg shells.

Egbe- A society formed by those of like nature to uphold a particular cause.

Egun- Spiritual entities that are attached or associated to someone often providing guidance, protection and healing.

Elekes- Sacred beaded necklaces of each orişa used as talismans.

Eşu- The orişa of the crossroads of life.

Ide- A bracelet worn as a talisman.

Iku- Death.

Ile- Land, house or home.

Irunmole- Orişas sent from the Upper Echelon to the Earth by the Almighty God, Olodumare to prepare for the birth of man. Man is a short word for
Man-ifestation of life in the physical form.
Woman is short for
Womb-manifestation of life in the physical form.

Iya- Mother.

Iyami- Female Mothers of the Night.

Iyaloşa- A female priest who has given birth to an orişa.

Lukumi/Lucumi- was an ancient area in Nigeria. Today it is a title given to the form of religious practice derived from Cuba.

Maferefun- A phrase giving thanks, gratitude and honor.

Meji-   Twin or two of a kind.

Moforibale- A salutation of honor.

Mojuba- A system of prayers in honor of all ascended beings in one's family line.

Oba-   A title given to a male priest of a particular status.

Obi-   A system of divination using coconut shells or ikin/ kola nuts.

Ochinchin- A cooked adimu dish to Oṣun using eggs, shrimp, greens, palm oil, honey.

Odu-   One of the Laws of Ifa and the Merindilogun.

Omo-   Child.

Opa-   Staff.

Opele-   Divining implement use by the Babalawo when casting to Ifa.

Opon-   Diving tray used by the Babalawo when casting to Ifa.

Ori-   The Destiny of one's Head.

Oriate-   A priest proficient in interpreting the odus and performing ritual ceremonies.

Oriki-   Prayers.

Orin-   Songs.

Oriṣa-   The Deities as Emissaries of the Almighty God Olodumare.

Orun-   Heaven.

Osa/ Oṣa- Initiation to the Oriṣa.

Osogbo- Negative influence.

Ota-   Sacred stones.

Pataki-   A folklore or story giving light to life's circumstances characterized by the oriṣa.

Santeria- A system of worship in Cuba of the saints syncretized with the orişa.

Şekere- A musical instrument made from a gourd or calabash.

Warriors- The group of orişas given for protection. They are: Elegba, Ogun, Ososi and Osain.

Yeye- Title used in reference to Oşun.

Yoruba- A tribe of people in Nigeria.

About the Author

As far back as she can remember Nia Jones-Morgan OṣunYami was involved in the arts. There was always a striving of balance and fullness of physical, mental and spiritual training. She studied Yoga and meditation in 1968 at Integral Yoga in New York City. This was the same year that she decided to add African dance classes to her 12 years of Modern dance training. The drums struck a chord in her spirit and she danced with Black Rose and Jesse Oliver for a number of years.

As a mother of three and a science student at City College of New York (CCNY), it was in 1973 that she also began studying as a Rosicrucian. In 1977 she commenced the study of The Kabala, Tarot, Herbalism and Spiritual Culture under Rojelio Straughn-Shekhem Ur Shekhem and in 1980 she was initiated into the priesthood of the Ausar Auset Society. After receiving a Bachelor of Science degree from CCNY, Ms. Jones-Morgan studied at the New York School of Shiatsu under Martin Ravitski, The New Age Center and the Harlem Institute of Traditional Chinese Medicine under M'tulu Shakur and Richard Delaney.

In 1986 she became the founder and director of the Brooklyn Center for the Healing Arts. That year brought on some challenges so she spent a short stay at the Oyotunji Village and received counsel from Oba Ofuntola Oserjiman Adelabu Adefumi I- (ibae t'orun). Three years later she was initiated as a priest of Oṣun in the Yoruba Lucumi religion by Deidre Lloyd- Oṣun Lade. Over the last 27 years Ms. Jones-Morgan studied Merindilogun with Alfred Davis- Omi Toki- (ibae t'orun) in 1994 & 2001, Barbara Bey- Ogun Relekun - (ibae t'orun)in 2002, Jose Manuel-Oya Dina (ibae t'orun) in 2003 and John Mason- Ofun Lade in 2006. She joined the Awo Oṣun Egbe in 1996 and sat on the Board of directors of Ijo Oriṣa in 1997.

For 23 years Ms. Jones-Morgan supervised a unit of child abuse and neglect investigators at The Administration for Children's Services. She received her Licensed Master of Social Work- LMSW degree from Fordham University. She is now retired and gracefully serves as a counselor, spiritual advisor and a wholistic practitioner living both in New York and Georgia.